HUNT FOR HECTOR

By
Anthony Tallarico

Incorporated

Copyright © 1989 Kidsbooks, Inc.
7004 N. California Ave
Chicago, Il 60645

ISBN: 0-942025-27-X

HUNT FOR HECTOR
AT THE DOG HALL
OF FAME
AND . . .

- ☐ Alien
- ☐ Astronaut
- ☐ Automobile
- ☐ Babe Ruff
- ☐ 2 Birds
- ☐ Boot
- ☐ "Buffalo Bull"
- ☐ Cannon
- ☐ Cat
- ☐ "Cave Dog"
- ☐ Clown
- ☐ Cook
- ☐ Doghouse
- ☐ "Down Boy"
- ☐ Elephant
- ☐ Fallen star
- ☐ Flying dog
- ☐ Football
- ☐ Ghost dog
- ☐ 2 Giant bones
- ☐ Guard dog
- ☐ Hot dog
- ☐ Husky
- ☐ Indian
- ☐ Juggler
- ☐ Kangaroo
- ☐ Man on leash
- ☐ Mirror
- ☐ Moon
- ☐ Mouse
- ☐ Napoleon
- ☐ Photographer
- ☐ Pilgrim
- ☐ Pirate flag
- ☐ Record player
- ☐ Santa hound
- ☐ Sheep
- ☐ Sherlock Bones
- ☐ Stamp
- ☐ Super hero
- ☐ Super poodle
- ☐ Target
- ☐ Tin can
- ☐ Umpire

HUNT FOR HECTOR AT DOG SCHOOL AND . . .

HUNT FOR HECTOR
AMONG THE DOG
CATCHERS
AND . . .

- ☐ Airplane
- ☐ Alien
- ☐ "Arf"
- ☐ Balloon
- ☐ Barber pole
- ☐ Carrots
- ☐ 5 Cats
- ☐ 3 Chimneys
- ☐ 3 Dog bowls
- ☐ 7 Dog catchers
- ☐ Doghouse
- ☐ Drums
- ☐ Firedogs
- ☐ 4 Fire hydrants
- ☐ Fisherdog
- ☐ 2 Flagpoles
- ☐ Flying saucer
- ☐ Gas mask
- ☐ 2 Howling dogs
- ☐ "Keep Things Clean"
- ☐ Mailbox
- ☐ Manhole cover
- ☐ 9 Police dogs
- ☐ 2 Restaurants
- ☐ Roadblock
- ☐ Rock and roll dog
- ☐ Santa dog
- ☐ Scout
- ☐ Shower
- ☐ Slice of pizza
- ☐ Streetlight
- ☐ 4 Super hero dogs
- ☐ Telephone
- ☐ Trail of money
- ☐ Trash can
- ☐ Tree
- ☐ 10 Trucks
- ☐ Turtle
- ☐ TV antenna
- ☐ TV camera
- ☐ Umbrella

HUNT FOR HECTOR
WHERE THE RICH
AND FAMOUS DOGS
LIVE AND . . .

- [ ] Admiral
- [ ] Alligator
- [ ] Artist
- [ ] Bank
- [ ] "Big Wheel"
- [ ] Bird bath
- [ ] Blimp
- [ ] Bone chimney
- [ ] Candle
- [ ] Castle
- [ ] Cat
- [ ] 2 Cooks
- [ ] Crown
- [ ] Dog fish
- [ ] Dog flag
- [ ] Dog prince statue
- [ ] 2 Dog-shaped bushes
- [ ] Door dog
- [ ] Fat dog
- [ ] Fire hydrant
- [ ] Fisherdog's catch
- [ ] 2 Golfers
- [ ] Guard
- [ ] Heart
- [ ] Heron
- [ ] High rise condos
- [ ] Human
- [ ] 3 Joggers
- [ ] 6 Limousines
- [ ] Periscope
- [ ] Pillow
- [ ] Pool
- [ ] Sipping a soda
- [ ] Star
- [ ] Tennis player
- [ ] TV antenna
- [ ] Umbrella
- [ ] Violinist
- [ ] Water-skier
- [ ] Whale

HUNT FOR HECTOR AT THE K-9 CLEANUP AND . . .

- ☐ Anchor
- ☐ Bath brush
- ☐ 3 Birds
- ☐ Bomb
- ☐ Broom
- ☐ 2 Burned out light bulbs
- ☐ Cannon
- ☐ Cat
- ☐ Coffin
- ☐ Dog bowl
- ☐ Doghouse
- ☐ Dog in disguise
- ☐ Elephant
- ☐ 4 Empty food cans
- ☐ 3 Fire hydrants
- ☐ Fire pig
- ☐ Fisherdog
- ☐ Flying fish
- ☐ Frankenswine
- ☐ Garbage can
- ☐ Horse
- ☐ Indian dog
- ☐ "K-8"
- ☐ Life preserver
- ☐ Lunch box
- ☐ Mermaid
- ☐ Mob spy
- ☐ Mouse
- ☐ Net
- ☐ Oil leak
- ☐ Old dog
- ☐ Old tire
- ☐ Palm tree
- ☐ Penguin
- ☐ Periscope
- ☐ Pighole cover
- ☐ Rabbit
- ☐ Rubber duck
- ☐ Sailor pig
- ☐ Skateboard
- ☐ Telescope
- ☐ Violin case

HUNT FOR HECTOR
AT THE SUPER
DOG BOWL
AND . . .

HUNT FOR HECTOR AT THE DOG OLYMPICS AND . . .

HUNT FOR HECTOR
AT THE TV QUIZ
SHOW
AND . . .

HUNT FOR HECTOR IN SPACE AND . . .

- ☐ Bark Vader
- ☐ Boat
- ☐ Boney Way
- ☐ Book
- ☐ Bow-wow land
- ☐ Boxing glove
- ☐ Cat
- ☐ Condo
- ☐ Dog catcher
- ☐ Dog graduate
- ☐ Dog trek
- ☐ Doggy bag
- ☐ Duck Rogers
- ☐ Emergency stop
- ☐ Fire hydrant
- ☐ Flying dog house
- ☐ Flying food dish
- ☐ Jail
- ☐ Kite
- ☐ Launch site
- ☐ Lost and found
- ☐ Mail carrier
- ☐ Map
- ☐ Moon dog
- ☐ "No Barking"
- ☐ Parachute
- ☐ Pirate
- ☐ Pizza
- ☐ Planet of the bones
- ☐ Planet of the dogs
- ☐ Police dog
- ☐ Pup tent
- ☐ Puppy trainer
- ☐ Robot dog
- ☐ Sleeping dog
- ☐ Space circus
- ☐ Surfboard
- ☐ Swimming pool
- ☐ Tire
- ☐ Unicycle
- ☐ Vampire dog
- ☐ Vanishing dog

HUNT FOR HECTOR IN DOGTOWN AND . . .

HUNT FOR HECTOR   SEARCH FOR SAM   FIND FREDDIE   LOOK FOR LISA